Magnetism and Electromagnets

Eve Hartman and Wendy Meshbesher

www.raintreepublishers.co.uk
Visit our website to find out more information about Raintree books.

To order:
Phone 44 (0) 1865 888112
Send a fax to 44 (0) 1865 314091
Visit the Raintree Bookshop at www.raintreepublishers.co.uk to browse our catalogue and order online.

Raintree is an imprint of Pearson Education Limited, a company incorporated in England and Wales having its registered office at Edinburgh Gate, Harlow, Essex, CM20 2JE – Registered company number: 00872828

First published in hardback in 2009

Edited by Megan Cotugno and Andrew Farrow
Designed by Philippa Jenkins
Original illustrations ©Pearson Education Ltd
Illustrated by KJA-artists.com
Picture research by Ruth Blair
Originated by Modern Age
Printed and bound in China by Leo Paper Group

ISBN 978 1 406210 77 4
13 12 11 10 09
10 9 8 7 6 5 4 3 2 1

British Library Cataloguing in Publication Data
A full catalogue record for this book is available from the British Library.

Acknowledgements
We would like to thank the following for allowing their pictures to be reproduced in this publication:
© Alamy/China Images p. **33**; © Alamy/Leslie Garland Picture Library p. **26**; © Alamy/Phil Degginger pp. **13**, **24**; © Alamy/Purple Marbles p. **19**; © Alamy/Leslie Garland Picture Library pp. **6**, **8**; © Art Directors/Trip p. **15**; © Corbis/Bettmann p. **23**; © Corbis/MedioImages p. **37**; © Corbis/Ralph White p. **22**; © iStockphoto/Ruud de Man p. **43**; © Pearson Education Ltd/Tudor Photography p. **5**; © Photodisc p. **iii** (Contents); © Photolibrary Group p. **4**; Photolibrary Group (re)view p. **36**; © Photolibrary Group/Alaskastock p. **iii** (Contents), **21**; © Photolibrary Group/IFA Animals p. **7**; © Photolibrary Group/phototake science p. **39**; © Science Photo Library pp. **34**, **35**; © Science Photo Library/Andrew Lambert Photography pp. **27**, **28**; © Science Photo Library/Centre Jean Perrin p. **38**; © Science Photo Library/Fermilab p. **17**; © Science Photo Library/U.S. Dept. of Energy p. **31**; © Shutterstock background images and design features throughout.

Cover photographs reproduced with permission of © Science Photo Library/Sovereign, ISM **main**; © Photolibrary Group/Phototake Science **inset**.

The publishers would like to thank literacy consultant Nancy Harris and content consultant John Pucek for their assistance in the preparation of this book.

Some words are shown in bold, like this. These words are explained in the glossary. You will find important information and definitions underlined, like this.

Contents

These colourful lights moving across the sky are actually caused by magnetism! Go to page 21 to read why!

How do magnets help doctors see inside a patient's brain? Find out on page 38!

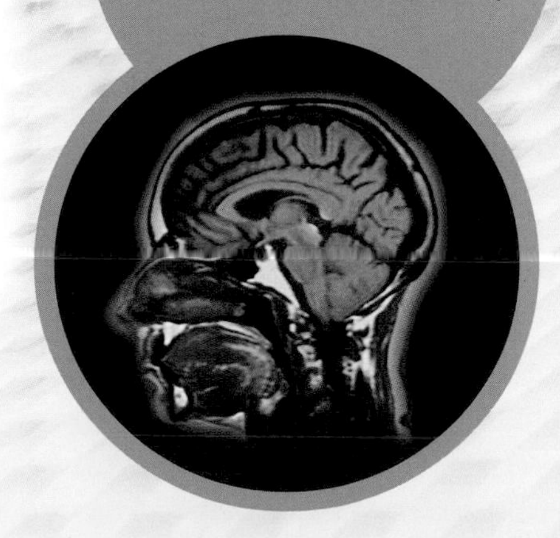

Magnetism

Look at the photograph below. What force holds up the scrap metal against the pull of gravity? The answer is magnetism. Magnetism is a force that pushes or pulls on certain metals. An object called a magnet can push or pull by using magnetism. An electric current acts like a magnet, too.

Some magnets are **permanent magnets**, meaning they will last a long time. Others are temporary, meaning their magnetic effect gradually weakens until it is lost. The metal disk that holds up the scrap metal is an example of an **electromagnet**. An electromagnet is a **temporary magnet** made by an electric current, which is a flow of **charged particles**.

A powerful electromagnet holds this scrap metal in the air. The magnet will work until the electricity is turned off.

Magnets in action

What happens if you pass a magnet through a mixture of different objects? A magnet attracts objects made of certain metals, and does not attract other objects. Steel and other **iron**-containing metals are attracted to magnets. Among the materials not attracted to magnets are paper, plastic, glass, cloth, and water.

As the photograph on the right shows, a magnet's effects can pass through objects stuck to it. This is why a chain of metal paper clips will dangle off a magnet. Each paper clip acts as a magnet to attract the next paper clip in the chain. If the top clip is pulled away, the chain will fall apart.

Have you ever seen a paper clip or other small object jump up to meet a magnet? This proves that magnetic force does not require touching. If a magnet is strong enough, an object could jump towards it through the air or move towards it through water.

The stronger the magnet, the more paper clips it can hold in a chain.

Where are magnets used?

You might use small magnets to hold messages to a refrigerator or to keep chess pieces on a metal board. Magnets are a part of many useful devices, including computers, televisions, and electric motors and generators. A compass needle is a magnet that can swing freely. Scientists think that some birds have a type of magnet inside them that acts like a compass and helps them find their way.

HOW DO MAGNETS WORK?

Magnetism is a property of the atoms of certain elements, among them iron, nickel, and cobalt. Elements are the simplest substances that make up the world around you. Atoms are the smallest pieces of elements.

History of magnets

Magnets have been known since ancient times. Around 600 CE, the Greeks discovered **lodestone**, a mineral that attracted metal. The Greeks discovered this mineral in a region of Turkey called **Magnesia**. The property of attracting metals became known as magnetism.

Lodestone may appear to be an ordinary rock. But as the Greeks discovered, it is one of the few natural magnetic minerals.

Independently of the Greeks, the ancient Chinese had discovered magnetic minerals, too. They also discovered some uses for them. They found that when a magnet swings freely, it always points in the same direction. This led them to invent the **magnetic compass**. By the 1100s, Chinese sailors were using compasses to navigate.

In 1600 English scientist William Gilbert explained why magnetic compasses worked. His answer was that Earth itself was magnetic! Later on in this book, you will learn why Gilbert was correct.

The magnetic elements

The magnetic elements are all metals. Iron is the most common magnetic element in everyday life. Iron makes up about 5 percent of Earth's **crust**.

What makes certain atoms magnetic? The reason lies in their arrangement of **electrons**. Electrons are the tiny, negatively charged particles that move about an atom. In atoms of magnetic elements, electrons are arranged in just the right way to create a magnetic force.

While iron is magnetic, many **compounds** made with iron are not magnetic. A compound is made from two or more elements that join together. **Rust**, for example, is a compound of iron and oxygen. Iron atoms lose their magnetism when they form rust.

In other compounds, iron keeps its magnetic properties. Lodestone, for example, is made of iron and oxygen, just as rust is. The iron remains magnetic because of lodestone's unique **crystal** structure. In a crystal, atoms are arranged in an orderly pattern.

Steel is magnetic. It is a mixture of iron, carbon, and other materials. In steel and other mixtures, iron atoms keep their magnetic properties.

A variety of magnets

A magnet can be made in almost any size or shape. You can find magnets in shapes such as bars, horseshoes, circles, cylinders, and spheres. Yet even if the magnet lacks two obvious ends, it still has two regions that act as a north **pole** and a south pole.

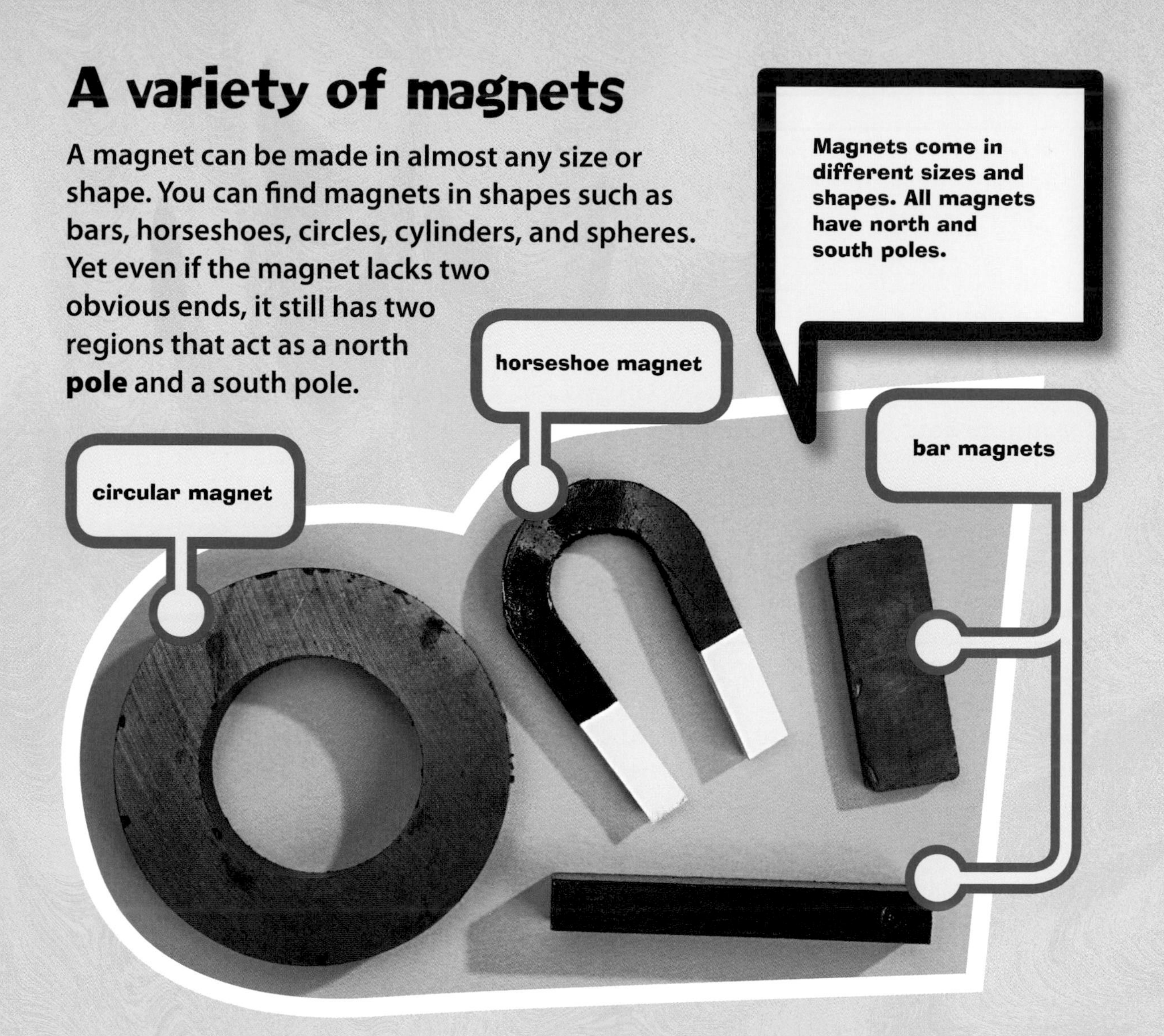

A magnet's attracting power is strongest at its poles. This fact explains why **horseshoe magnets** are popular. A horseshoe magnet is a **bar magnet** bent into the shape of the letter "U". In a bar magnet, the poles lie at opposite ends. The horseshoe shape brings the two poles of the magnet close together, making the magnet more powerful.

Some magnets are small enough to fit in the palm of your hand. But at Florida State University in the United States, scientists use magnets larger than your whole body! The university is home to the National High Magnetic Field Laboratory (Magnet Lab). The unusually large and powerful magnets help scientists from all sorts of fields, including life science, earth science, and physical science.

Two poles

Every magnet has two regions where the magnetic force is strongest. The regions are called the north pole and the south pole.

Bring two magnets together at their poles, and the magnetic force will always push or pull in the same way. Opposite poles from two magnets will attract each other, and like poles will repel. This means that the two magnets that attract will pull closer, and the two magnets that repel will push away. The diagrams show how pairs of poles attract and repel.

A magnet can never have only one pole. For example, you might think that cutting a bar magnet in half would separate its two poles. But amazingly, two new poles would form along the cut end! This would make two small bar magnets, each with a north pole and a south pole.

Magnetic forces from even a small bar magnet can be very strong. To see this for yourself, try bringing the south poles of two bar magnets together. You'll see that doing this is extremely difficult!

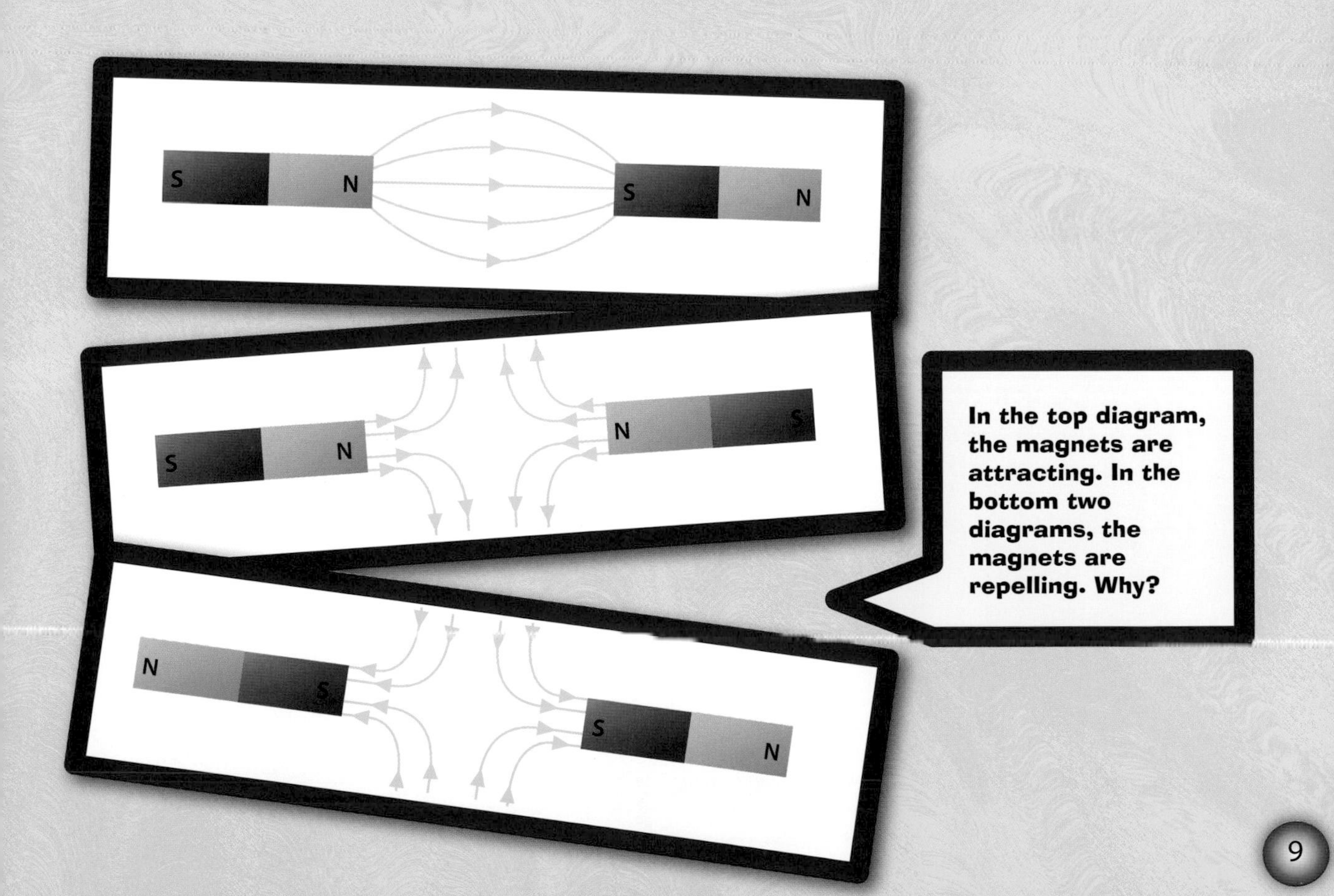

MAGNETIC DOMAINS

Iron atoms are a part of **permanent magnets**. Yet they are also a part of objects that do not act as magnets, such as a nail or a steel bridge. Why is a nail or bridge not magnetic? Scientists use the idea of **magnetic domains** to answer this question.

Remember that even the smallest magnet, such as an iron atom, has two poles. When iron atoms group together, the two poles of one atom force the poles of neighbour atoms to align the same way. This forms a region called a magnetic domain. The atoms in a magnetic domain are aligned magnetically. In this way, a magnetic domain acts like a tiny magnet.

Anything made of iron contains magnetic domains. Yet in an ordinary nail or other non-magnetic object, the north-south poles of the domains point in many directions. While each domain does act like a magnet, in total the effects cancel out one another.

In a permanent magnet, the poles in each domain point in the same direction. Thus, the magnetism of many domains is combined.

In these drawings, each bubble-shaped region is a magnetic domain. In a permanent magnet, the domains are aligned in the same direction.

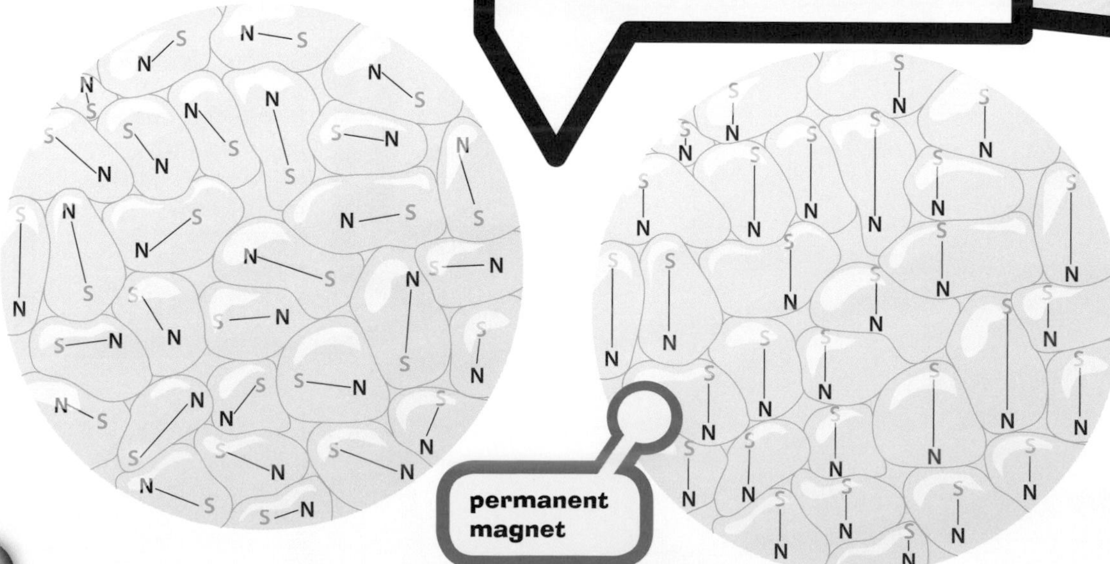

MAKE YOUR OWN MAGNET

Can you change an ordinary piece of metal into a magnet? Yes! Follow the directions in the activity below.

To explain why this activity works, review the illustrations of magnetic domains on page 10. In an ordinary piece of metal, the magnetic domains are not aligned and the iron is not magnetic. But when the metal is stroked on a permanent magnet, its domains align themselves. This changes the metal into a **temporary magnet**. The more it is stroked, the stronger and longer-lasting the temporary magnet becomes.

How to make a temporary magnet

Materials: Nail, screw, or other piece of metal; bar magnet; metal paper clips

1. Use the paper clips to test the magnetic properties of the piece of metal and the bar magnet. Record how many paper clips each can pick up.

2. Stroke the piece of metal 10 times against the bar magnet. Repeat Step 1.

3. Continue stroking the piece of metal. Find out how strong a magnet it will become, and how long the magnetism lasts.

Safety: Be careful when handling any sharp piece of metal.

MAGNETIC FIELDS

As you have read, the force of magnetism affects certain metals. Far away from the magnet, this force is very weak. Move closer, however, and the force becomes stronger, especially near the magnet's poles. A magnetic field is the area in which a magnet's pull has an effect. It is strongest at the poles. The more powerful a magnet, the larger the magnetic field around it.

Describing magnetic fields

To describe a magnetic field, scientists use drawings like the ones shown to the right. The field is represented by lines and arrows. The arrows always point from the north pole to the south pole. Where lines are closer together, such as near the poles, the field is stronger. Lines spread farther apart show where the field is weaker.

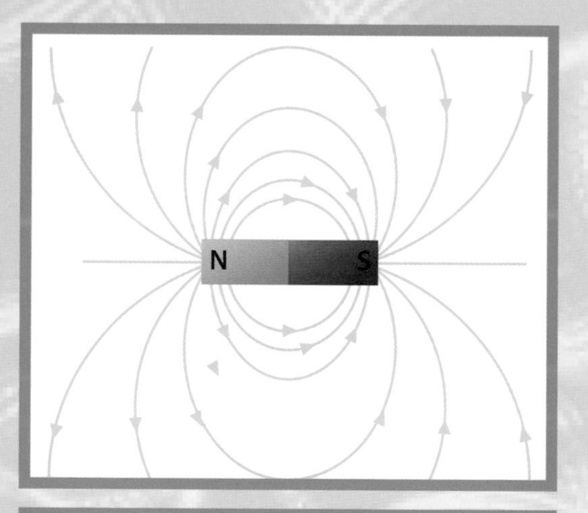

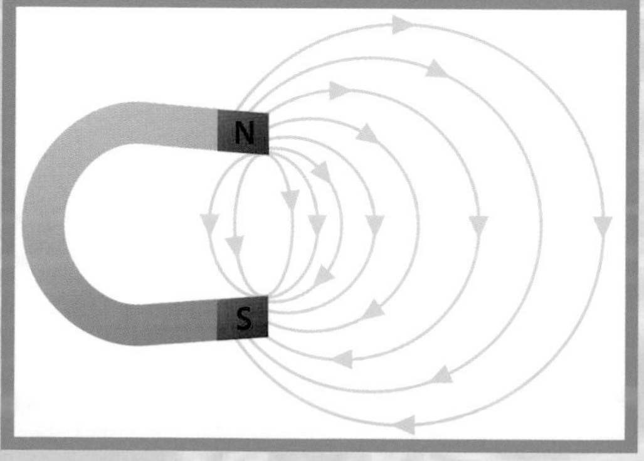

A good way to see a magnetic field in action is to spread **iron** filings around a magnet. Iron filings are small, thin pieces of iron, much like pencil shavings. When iron filings are placed around a magnet, each aligns along a line of the magnetic field. As the photograph on page 13 shows, the filings form a pattern that matches the magnetic field lines.

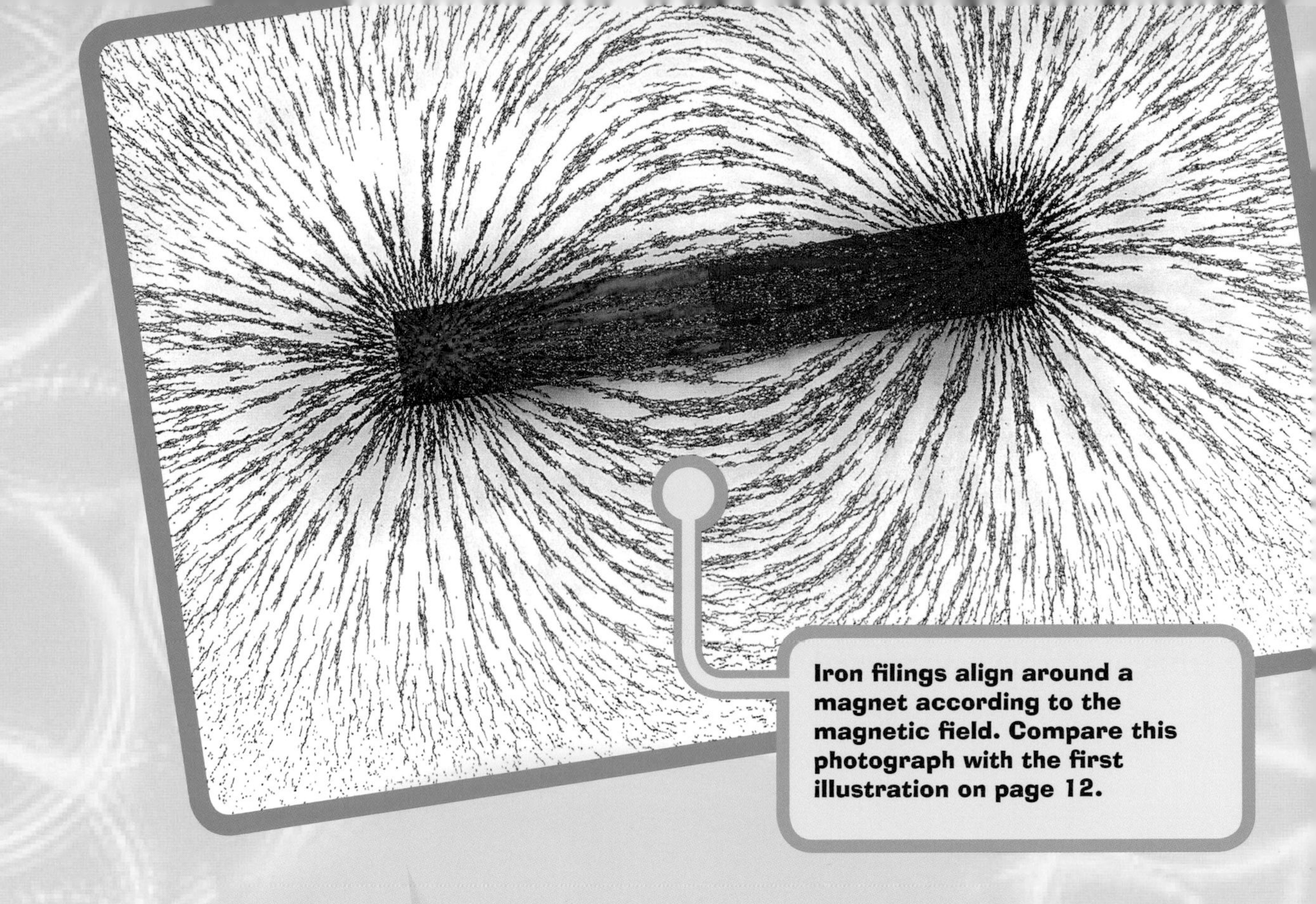

Iron filings align around a magnet according to the magnetic field. Compare this photograph with the first illustration on page 12.

The magnetic compass

How can you detect a magnetic field? One simple way is to use a **magnetic compass**. The needle of a compass is a thin **bar magnet** that can swing freely about its centre. In the presence of another magnetic field, the needle will swing so it aligns with that field. Its north-seeking pole will point north, and the south-seeking pole will point south.

If you move any **permanent magnet** near a compass, the needle will swing to point either towards or away from the magnet. But even if no magnets are near, the needle will always point in the same direction – north.

Stop the field

Will a forceful magnet pull underwater, or through paper or plastic? Scientists have tested many materials inside magnetic fields. They have yet to discover anything that will completely stop magnetism. Magnetic fields travel through solid, liquid, gas, and empty space. Even an ordinary magnet will pull things through a drinking glass, which is a solid, or water, which is a liquid.

Although a magnetic field cannot be unmade or eliminated, it can be contained. This effect is called **magnetic shielding**. Place a magnet inside an iron box, for example, and the magnetic field will stay mainly inside the box. The reason is because iron, like other materials that are easily magnetized, will "gather in" a magnetic field around it.

Destroying a magnet

It is not easy to destroy a permanent magnet. You could cut it into tiny pieces, but each piece would continue to be magnetic. Mix those pieces with other materials, and their magnetism would still remain. Painting a magnet, wrapping it in plastic, dipping it in water: none of these actions will undo the magnetic properties.

However, French scientist Pierre Curie discovered one way to destroy a magnet. When a magnetic metal is heated above a certain temperature, it loses its magnetic properties. This temperature is now called the **Curie Point**. For iron, the Curie Point is 770° Celsius (1,418° Fahrenheit). This is hotter than most household ovens ever become.

Mu-metal

If you need to shield the effects of a magnet, the best choice is a material called **mu-metal**. Mu-metal is a mixture of iron, **nickel**, and other metals. It is named after the Greek letter μ, pronounced "mew".

Mu-metal almost completely shields a magnetic field. This makes it useful in any device that uses magnets for very precise tasks. In later chapters, you will read about two of these devices: a computer's hard drive and a machine for **magnetic resonance imaging (MRI)**.

lectricity makes magnetic fields

As you read, the arrangement of **electrons** in certain metals causes magnetism. In addition, electrons can cause magnetism in other ways. An **electric current** is the flow of electrons or other **charged particles**. These electrons also create a magnetic effect. An electric current creates a circle-shaped magnetic field around the current's path.

To picture this field, place your right hand in the air, palm facing forward. Now curl forward four fingers (not the thumb) so they form a nearly closed circle. Hold that position as you imagine an electric current moving in the direction that your thumb points. The four curled fingers show the direction of the magnetic field.

lectric fields

An electric current creates not only a magnetic field, but an **electric field** as well. An electric field is the area surrounding the electric charge. Scientists describe the electric field and magnetic field together as an **electromagnetic field**. This kind of field is all around you, and any device that runs on electricity contributes to it. Light is a form of energy that travels as a wave through an electromagnetic field.

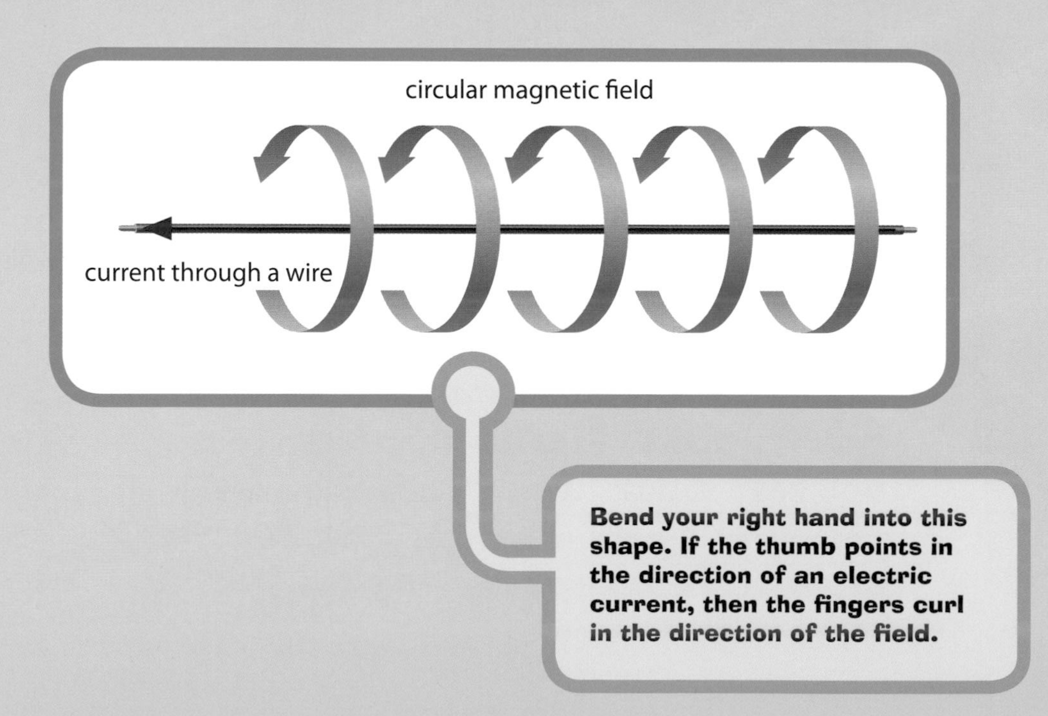

Bend your right hand into this shape. If the thumb points in the direction of an electric current, then the fingers curl in the direction of the field.

Measuring magnetic fields

Today, the strength of a magnetic field is measured in units called teslas (T), named after Austrian scientist Nikola Tesla. Also used are units called Gauss (G), named after another scientist, Johann Gauss.

The magnets you use at school have a field strength of a small fraction of one tesla. In comparison, the Magnet Lab at Florida State University in the United States has a magnet of 45 teslas strength. That's strong enough to send a hammer flying out of your hand – not that the scientists there would let this happen!

This large magnet has a magnetic field that is very strong. It is also potentially dangerous. Everyday magnets are much weaker and quite safe.

Earth as a magnet

Did you know at the very centre of Earth are two layers? This is called the core. The core is made of iron and nickel.

Remember that both iron and nickel are magnetic. Earth acts as a giant **magnet** because of the large amounts of iron and nickel in Earth's core. **Earth's magnetic field explains why compasses work. It also explains a beautiful effect called an aurora.** **You will learn more about this on page 21.**

Where are Earth's poles?

The term "pole" applies not only to magnets, but to Earth as a planet. Earth's **geographic poles** are called the North Pole and the South Pole. They are the ends of Earth's axis. Earth rotates, or spins, about on its axis, which is why Earth cycles between day and night.

Yet, Earth also acts as a magnet. As the diagram shows, Earth has a magnetic north pole and magnetic south pole, but perhaps not where you expect them to be. Earth's **magnetic poles** are in opposite positions to the geographic poles. Earth's magnetic south pole lies very close to the North Pole. Earth's magnetic north pole lies very close to the South Pole.

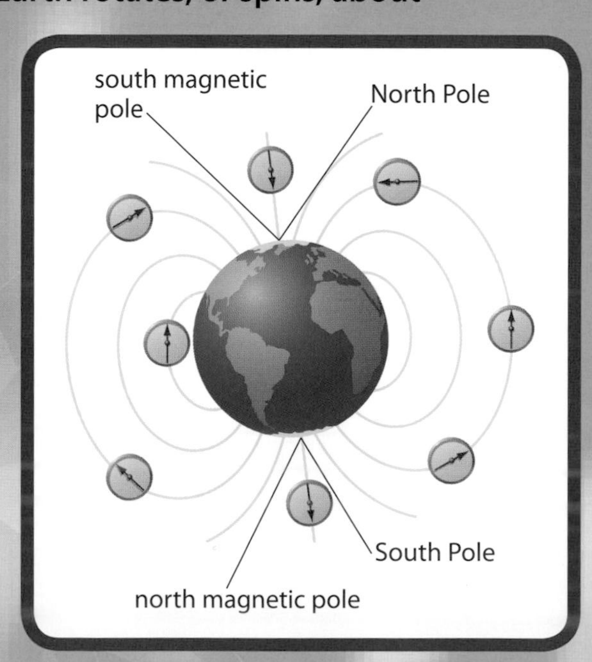

The compass

As you read earlier, a compass is a simple, useful tool for detecting magnetic fields. Its needle is a thin **bar magnet**. A compass needle points north because it aligns with Earth's magnetic field. The north pole of the needle points towards Earth's south magnetic pole.

Numbers or letters are printed around the face of a compass to show direction. The four main directions are north (N), east (E), south (S), and west (W). Many compasses also use the degree system for measuring direction. A full circle has 360 degrees, so north is equal to both 0° and 360°. East is 90°, south is 180°, and west is 270°.

For much of human history, compasses were widely used to help travellers find their way. Today, people still use compasses on hikes. Yet compasses have mainly been replaced by new, more accurate tools and technologies. The **Global Positioning System (GPS)** uses **radio waves** and a system of satellites. It can locate your position on Earth within a few metres!

thin bar magnet

Earth's metal core creates a huge magnetic field around the planet. A compass works because its needle aligns to this field.

True North?

A compass needle does not truly point to Earth's North Pole. The reason is that Earth's magnetic field is aligned closely to Earth's axis, but not exactly. Today, the south magnetic pole lies in far northern Canada, within a region around the North Pole called the Arctic Circle. For typical compass use, however, any error in its direction is too small to make a difference.

For reasons scientists do not fully understand, the positions of Earth's magnetic poles change slightly from year to year. For long spans of time in the distant past, magnetic north and south switched positions! As you will discover, this unusual fact led to some important discoveries about Earth's history.

Earth's magnetosphere

Earth's magnetic field does not stop at the surface. In fact, it reaches thousands of kilometres into space! The field helps form a region of space around Earth called the **magnetosphere**. Inside Earth's magnetosphere, tiny particles are trapped by forces of **magnetism** and electricity. Some of these particles come from the Sun, some come from elsewhere in space, and others escaped from Earth's upper atmosphere.

Despite its name, the magnetosphere does not form the shape of a sphere. It is somewhat ball-shaped on the side that faces the Sun. The other side, however, extends far off into space, forming a shape much like a cylinder.

Auroras look like ribbons of coloured light in the night sky. Although most common in polar regions, such as Alaska, a few have been spotted as far south as California and Texas in the United States.

Auroras

Some of the Sun's energy reaches Earth in the form of heat and light. The Sun also sends out a stream of tiny **charged particles**.

Normally, Earth's magnetosphere acts like an invisible shield against the solar wind. Sometimes, however, this shielding puts on quite a light show! When the solar wind is unusually strong, Earth's atmosphere and magnetosphere create a ribbon of lights called an aurora. Auroras are typically seen in polar regions, where the magnetic field is strongest.

Auroras are a sign of a magnetic storm, a temporary change in Earth's magnetic field. Severe magnetic storms can also disrupt **electrical transformers** and radio communications. Most storms last a day or two.

The rock file

In the 1950s, scientists began studying the deep ocean floor. They found iron **compounds** in the rocks, which was not surprising. They also found that within each rock, all the iron was magnetically aligned. That also was not surprising. Hot **lava** cooled to form the rocks, and the iron **atoms** aligned with Earth's magnetic field as it solidified.

The scientists also discovered that the rocks formed alternating bands along a chain of **volcanoes** called the **mid-ocean ridge**. In one band, the iron pointed north, while in the next it pointed south. This was very surprising! Rocks from the ocean floor show that Earth's magnetic field has reversed position many times, meaning its north and south poles switched places. The discovery also led to the theory of **tectonic plates**, which states that huge slabs of Earth move about its surface.

Rocks on the deep ocean floor are filled with iron compounds.

Alfred Wegener: studying magnetism in Earth's crust

Look at a map of the world. Can you see that Africa and South America have matching coastlines? In 1912 German scientist Alfred Wegener proposed a simple theory. His idea was that the continents were at one time joined together. They then drifted apart to their current positions. Wegener died long before most of his ideas were proven correct.

Alfred Wegener proposed that Earth's crust moved across the planet.

EARTH'S MAGNETIC HISTORY!

- Earth's magnetic field has reversed about 170 times over the last 100 million years.
- Some scientists predict that Earth's magnetic field will reverse again in about 2,000 years.
- Mid-ocean ridges rise from the middle of every ocean. They roughly trace the boundaries of nearby continents.
- Dinosaurs once roamed between the Appalachian Mountains of North America and the Scottish Highlands of Great Britain. These two mountain ranges were once connected!

ELECTRICITY AND MAGNETISM

As you read earlier, an electric current creates a magnetic field around it. People apply this fact to make a temporary yet powerful magnet called an electromagnet. An electromagnet is made by wrapping coils of electric current around a piece of metal containing iron. The magnetic field of the wire acts to magnetize the metal piece inside the loops.

An electromagnet may be as simple as the nail and wire shown here. A large electromagnet may be powerful enough to lift a car. Electromagnets are also found in devices such as televisions, computers, **motors**, and **generators**.

Wrapping coils of electrical wire around a nail can change it into an electromagnet.

Solenoids

A single wire wrapped into a cylinder-shaped coil is called a **solenoid**. The solenoid is key to the strength of the electromagnet. The more tightly the solenoid is wound, the stronger the electromagnet becomes.

Why should solenoids create such a powerful magnetic field? To picture the answer, imagine that you are sitting on an iron bar in the centre of an electromagnet. Electric current is circling in the solenoid around you. With every circle, that electric current is adding to the magnetic field where you are. That is much more powerful than if the current merely passed by in a straight line.

Properties of electromagnets

In most ways, an electromagnet acts just like any other magnet. An electromagnet has a north **pole** and a south pole, and it attracts only iron and a few other metals. Its magnetic field is quite strong, but otherwise behaves just like the field from a typical **bar magnet**.

Unlike a **permanent magnet**, an electromagnet can be easily controlled. Its strength depends on the strength of the current through the solenoid. The strength of an electromagnet can be changed, either gradually or quickly, by changing the electric current.

Using electromagnets

As you have seen, electromagnets are powerful tools for lifting objects that contain iron, such as the frames of old cars. However, electromagnets are part of all sorts of devices. Most of these devices make use of the way magnets and electrical current affect one another. Here are two examples:

Sound speakers

You might listen to music from a radio or a television set, from a CD player, or from a digital player that fits in your pocket! All of these devices rely on speakers. A speaker changes a coded message in an electrical current into sounds you can hear.

A speaker uses two magnets: a permanent magnet and a moveable electromagnet inside it. Electric current travels through the wire loops of the electromagnet. As that current changes, the magnetic field of the electromagnet becomes slightly stronger or weaker. This moves the electromagnet back and forth slightly. This motion, in turn, makes the speaker cone vibrate. You hear those vibrations as sound.

As an electric current changes, the strength and direction of the magnetic field also changes. The electromagnet moves back and forth to set the speaker cone vibrating.

Television sets

Until recently, most television sets used a device called a **cathode ray tube (CRT)**. A cathode is a source of **electrons**. In a CRT, the cathode sends a thin electron beam towards a screen. The screen is made of tiny coloured dots that glow when the beam strikes them.

Without parts to guide it, the ray would strike only the centre of the screen. So wrapped around the back of a CRT is an electromagnet. As current changes through the electromagnet, the electron beam moves either up and down or back and forth in the changing magnetic field. The changes happen so quickly that images on the screen appear almost real!

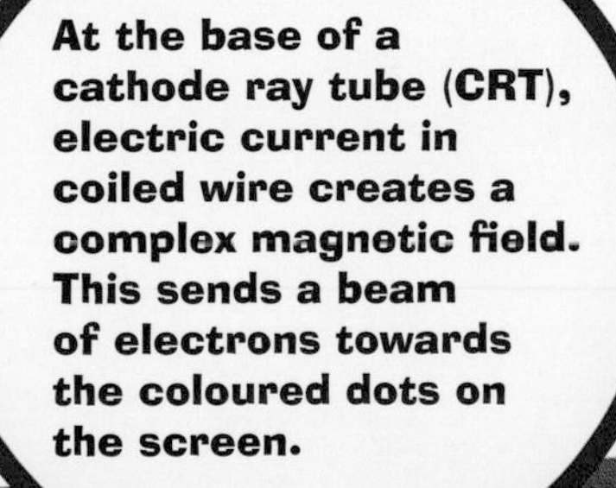

At the base of a cathode ray tube (CRT), electric current in coiled wire creates a complex magnetic field. This sends a beam of electrons towards the coloured dots on the screen.

Goodbye CRTs?

One drawback of CRTs is their size. The larger the picture screen, the longer the CRT must be to reach the screen's corners. This is why most new televisions are made with **plasma screens**. A plasma screen of any size needs to be only a few centimetres deep.

Motors and generators

An electric current, or electricity, is the movement of electrons or other electric charges. Electricity is a form of energy, and it is very useful because it can travel long distances. It may travel hundreds of kilometres from a power plant to your home.

How is electricity made? How can it be used to run devices such as refrigerators, washing machines, and even electric pencil sharpeners? The answers to these questions involve **magnets**. Magnets can be used to help change the energy of motion into electricity, and back again. The two types of devices that accomplish these tasks are **motors** and **generators**. Let's take a close look at each.

Inside a motor, the changing polarity of the electromagnet keeps the rotor spinning.

MOTORS

An electric motor uses two magnets, typically a **permanent magnet** (or a field magnet, as labelled in the diagram) and an **electromagnet**. Inside a motor, a pair of magnets help change electrical energy into the energy of motion. That motion is used to turn an axle, which is a cylinder-shaped rod.

As the diagram shows, the electromagnet is part of a rotor, which means it can spin. When the current is turned on, the rotor will spin so that the north **pole** of the electromagnet is aligned to the south pole of the permanent magnet. (Even if the motor lacked other parts, the rotor would stay in this position!)

Now, look closely at the brushes and the commutator. As the rotor spins, these parts keep switching the direction of the current through the electromagnet. As the current switches, so too does the polarity of the electromagnet. Sometimes the north pole is at one end, sometimes it is at the other end. This keeps the rotor spinning in the **magnetic field**, and that turns the axle.

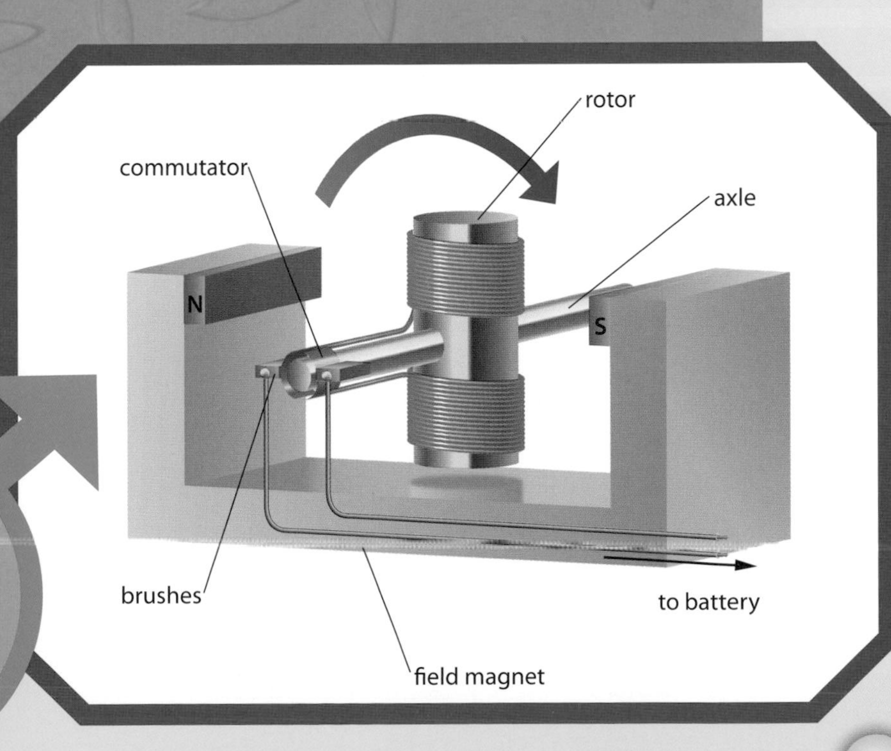

Take a close look at how the electric motor works. Two magnets help keep it running.

Generators

As you read on page 16, an electric current in a wire creates a magnetic field around it. In addition, the reverse process can also happen: a magnetic field will create an electric current in a moving wire. This fact is put to good use in a device called a generator.

A generator uses magnets to change the energy of motion into electricity. This means that a generator performs the opposite task of a motor. In fact, some motors can be easily converted into generators, and vice versa!

In a simple generator, an energy source is used to turn a loop of wire between two poles of a magnet. As the loop turns, sometimes one side is near the north pole and sometimes it is near the south pole. The loop's motion in the magnetic field creates an electric current inside it. The ends of the loop connect to metal rings, which lead to an electric circuit.

Small generators

Most homes and businesses use electricity from large **power plants**. You will read more about power plants on the next page. Yet many people buy and use small generators. They are useful on camping trips or for outdoor parties. Most run on either petrol or diesel fuel.

Most large hospitals keep their own generators. If the normal power supply fails – during a thunderstorm, for example – the generators are turned on so that important equipment keeps running.

Power plants

Huge, powerful generators are put to use at power plants. A power plant is the source of the electricity for your home, school, and community. Power plants may run on a variety of energy sources. Such sources include coal or other fossil fuels, rushing water in a river, steady winds, and heat from Earth's interior. The fuel for a nuclear power plant is uranium. This is a metal that naturally radiates or gives off energy.

Regardless of the energy source, all power plants typically use the same steps for generating electricity. All rely on the same kind of generators.

You can see the powerful generators in this room at a nuclear power plant.

Magnets and motion

If you roll a toy car across the floor, gradually it will slow down and stop. The reason is friction. Friction is a force that acts in the opposite direction of motion. It is caused when things rub against one another, such as a car's tyres and the road. Even air causes friction.

To make things travel as fast as possible, engineers look for ways to keep friction low. Because magnets work without touching, they can make things move very fast, with little or no friction. This principle explains why the world's fastest trains use magnets to run.

Maglev trains

The word "maglev" comes from **magnetic levitation**. To levitate is to rise up into the air and float with no support. A maglev train uses magnets to separate from its track and move forwards at high speeds. The separation may be as little as 15 millimetres (0.6 inch), which is not very much. However, it is enough to eliminate friction with the track.

All maglev trains use two magnets: one inside the train and one on the track. Some trains are designed so that the two magnets repel each other. These trains lift up from their tracks. Other trains are designed to use attractive forces of magnets. These trains hang below the tracks. In both types of trains, the track just in front of the train is changed into a powerful **electromagnet**. This pulls the train forwards.

The fastest speed recorded for a maglev train is 581 kph (361 mph). It is the fastest train ever!

Find out on page 42 how to make your own maglev!

Maglevs in the future

Scientists have been studying the idea of maglev for at least 70 years. Yet, only a few maglev train lines have ever been built, and even fewer are still running. Most of today's maglev trains are in China and Japan.

The main drawback of maglev is its expense. The maglev train line in Shanghai, China, covers a little over 30 kilometres (19 miles) but cost millions of pounds to build. However, the maglev has many advantages, too. They run on electricity, not on fossil fuels as most cars and aeroplanes do. With some new breakthroughs in technology, maybe a maglev train will serve your community some day.

Maglev trains are extremely fast, as well as very quiet. However, they are also expensive to build and run.

Particle accelerators

How can you find out what something is made of? One way is to break it apart and study the pieces. This is the main job of a particle accelerator. A particle accelerator uses magnets and electricity to speed up atoms and other tiny particles. It then contains or crushes them. With the help of particle accelerators, scientists have learned many surprising facts about atoms and matter.

A very simple particle accelerator is a **cathode ray tube (CRT)**, which you studied on page 27. In a CRT, the particles are **electrons**, which travel in a beam from the back of the CRT to the screen. Magnets are used to direct the electron beam.

While a CRT is about as long as your arm, the particle accelerator at Stanford University in the United States is 3 kilometres (2 miles) long. Other accelerators carry particles through circular tubes. Inside them, particles can travel endlessly before they are released.

Steering these high-speed particles requires some very powerful magnets. In fact, a new particle accelerator in Geneva, Switzerland, called the Large Hadron Collider, uses the world's most powerful electromagnet. This magnet is the size of a house and weighs about 1,800 tonnes!

This particle accelerator in Switzerland uses the most powerful electromagnet in the world.

This is an end view of one of the magnets that is part of the Large Hadron Collider.

Uses for particle accelerators

Particle accelerators have many uses. At hospitals, **X-rays** are typically made from particle accelerators. Doctors and dentists use X-rays to study bones, teeth, and other hidden parts of the body.

Scientists are using the world's largest particle accelerators to answer all sorts of questions. What particles make up an atom? What particles make up the universe? Just how did the universe begin, and what will happen to it next? These questions, and others like them, may someday have new, exciting answers.

Magnets and information

As you read on page 22, scientists have found that iron in Earth's rocks can hold magnetic information.

Scientists can also use iron to make magnetic storage devices. In magnetic storage devices, iron-containing compounds record and store information. The information is coded by a changing magnetic field. These storage devices include magnetic tape and the hard disks of computers.

Magnetic recording

In 1898 Danish scientist Valdemar Poulsen invented the first magnetic recording device. This invention used a thin wire that moved past either a recording head or a play-back head. At the recording head, the wire was magnetized according to an electrical signal. The signal was coded from sound waves. At the play-back head, the magnetic pattern on the wire was translated back into electricity, then into the original sounds.

This reel-to-reel tape recorder dates from the 1950s. It used magnetic heads both to record patterns on the tape and to read those patterns.

Patterns of magnetism can store information on magnetic tape, magnetic stripes in credit cards, and many other magnetic objects. What other uses for magnetic recording can you think of?

Magnetic stripes are used to store information on hotel keys, credit cards, and passes for the underground.

Computer hard drives

A computer uses magnetic devices to store information. The main storage device of a computer is called a hard drive. Like magnetic tape, a hard drive is coated in magnetic material that stores information. Look back at the picture on page 15. This is a hard drive, and it is coated in the magnetic material, **Mu-metal**.

Magnetic Resonance Imaging

In 1977 a team of American physicians and scientists invented a new way to take pictures of the inside of the human body. Their technique is now called **magnetic resonance imaging**, or **MRI**. In MRI, **radio waves** and powerful **magnets** scan the insides of the body. They study one tiny piece at a time. A computer then shows how the pieces fit together. The result is a very detailed and useful picture.

MRI uses the hydrogen in the human body. Hydrogen is a very common **element**. It is part of nearly every **compound** that living things make or use.

A magnetic field will not attract or repel hydrogen **atoms**. However, under the proper conditions, it will cause temporary changes to the atoms' central cores, or **nuclei**. An MRI machine can detect these changes and use them to make an image.

Uses for MRI

Doctors order an MRI scan to help diagnose all sorts of diseases and injuries. MRI can detect changes in body parts very difficult to reach otherwise, such as deep inside the brain. It can show both hard parts, such as bones, and soft parts, such as blood vessels and the blood inside them. It can also show the extent of damage to joints.

An MRI scan presents no danger to the patient, and side effects of any kind are rare. Its main drawback is cost. An MRI machine is expensive to purchase, and a scan may take an hour or longer.

This clear image of the brain was obtained by using an MRI machine.

INSIDE AN MRI MACHINE

An MRI machine looks like a box with a cylinder-shaped hole inside it. The magnetic field runs through the cylinder, where the patient lies inside.

An MRI scan is not painful or uncomfortable, but neither is it pleasant. The patient must hold still inside a small space throughout the scan. The machine is very noisy, too. Many patients wear ear plugs. However, most patients agree that the benefits of MRI are worth the effort.

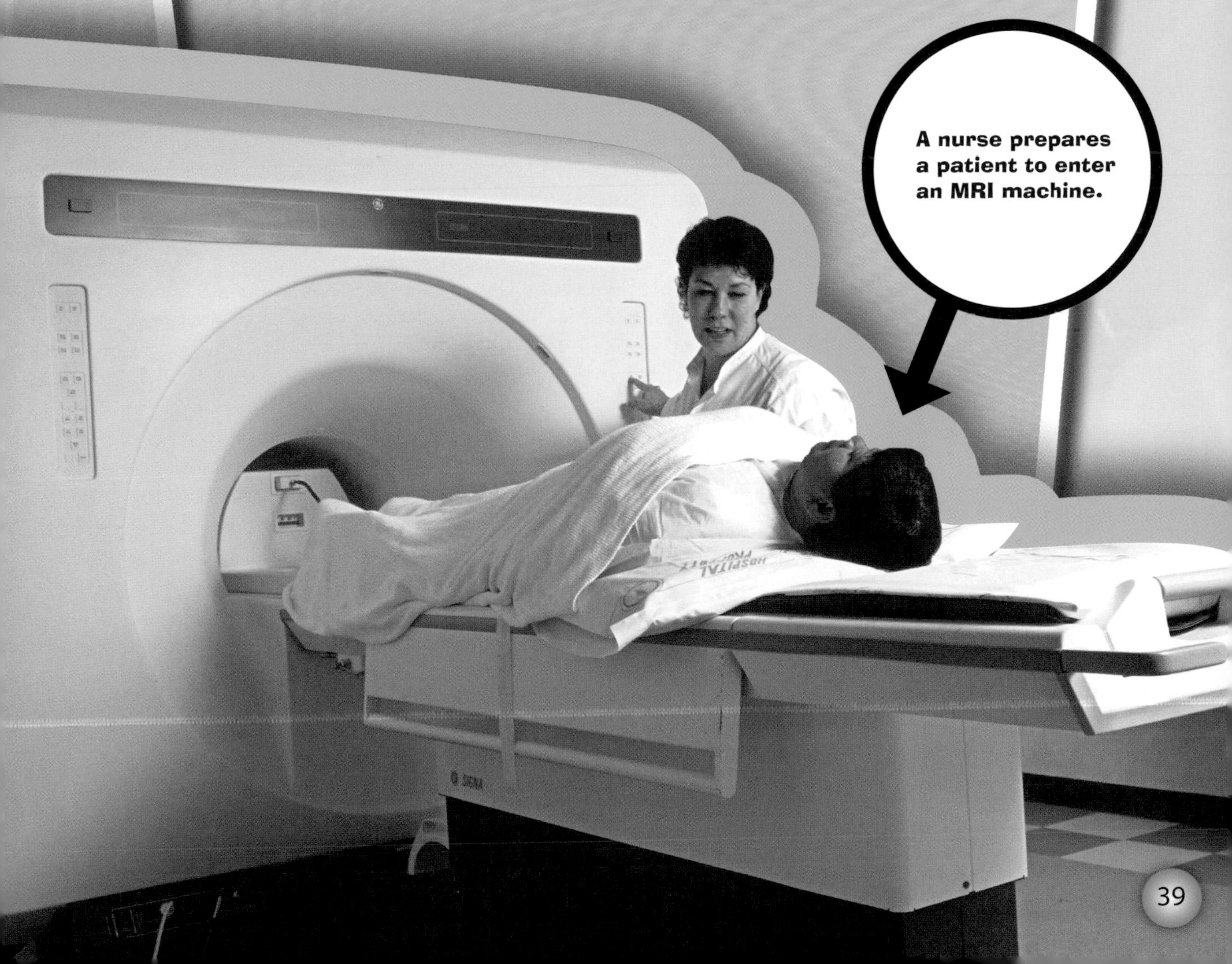

A nurse prepares a patient to enter an MRI machine.

Magnet mixture

Materials:

Bar magnet; objects such as paper clips, nails, drawing pins, marbles, broken crayons, and pencils

1. Mix all of the objects together.
2. Slowly pass the magnet among the mixture. Make sure it touches all of the objects at least once.
3. Divide the objects into two groups based on whether the magnet attracted them. Describe how the two groups are different.

What can you do with magnets? The answers may surprise you! Get permission from an adult, then try the rest of the projects.

A SIMPLE MOTOR

Materials for building a simple motor are sold in kits at hobby stores and toy stores. However, the world's simplest motor needs only four parts, all easy to obtain. Follow the directions shown here.

Materials:

Battery, electrical wire, iron-containing screw or nail, and a small disk-shaped magnet (neodymium is ideal)

1. Attach the magnet to the flat end of the screw or nail.
2. Dangle the sharp end of the screw or nail below the negative terminal of the battery. (Magnetic attraction should hold it there.)
3. Touch one end of the wire to the positive terminal of the battery. Touch the other end against the edge of the magnet. Observe the results.
4. Predict what will happen if you reverse the polarity of the current, meaning you exchange the positive and negative terminals in Step 2 and Step 3. Test your prediction.

This device is called a homopolar motor. It differs from most motors because current runs through the permanent magnet, making it an electromagnet as well. The spinning force comes from the interaction of the two magnetic fields.

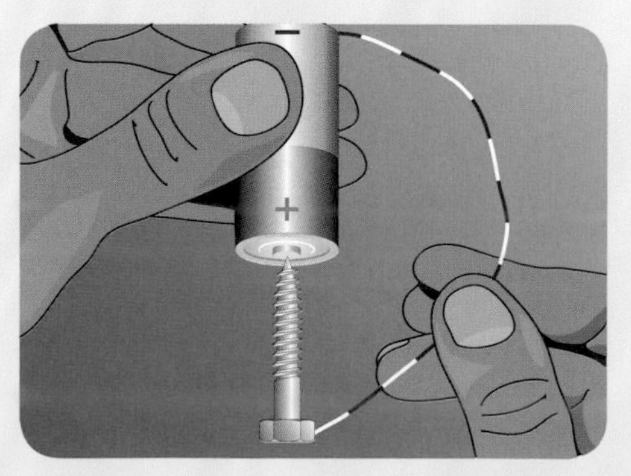

THE SNOWFLAKE CHALLENGE

Magnetism is an invisible force, and sometimes people do not expect it. Use a magnetic snowflake to challenge your friends and family.

Materials:

A glass jar with lid, a small magnet, tape, string (very thin and lightweight), 3 metal paper clips, tissue paper, dark-coloured construction paper

1. Tape the magnet to the bottom of the jar. Tape construction paper over the magnet to hide it.
2. Cut a small square of tissue paper into a snowflake or other shape. Hide paper clips under a fold or in a corner of the snowflake.
3. Use string to dangle the snowflake below the jar lid. The snowflake should come near to, but not touch, the bottom of the jar and the hidden magnet.
4. Slowly turn the jar upside down. The magnet should hold the snowflake in place. If not, rearrange the paper clips or add more paper clips.
5. When you are ready, repeat Step 4 for a friend, a family member, or a young child. Challenge him or her to explain why the snowflake hangs in the air.

Find the field

Materials:
Four sheets of construction paper, tape, bar magnet, metal paper clip

1. Tape four sheets of construction paper into one long, wide sheet. Tape the bar magnet face down at the centre.
2. Place the paper clip at different points on the sheet and let it go. At each point, draw the letter X if the paper clip moved towards the bar magnet. Draw an O if the paper clip did not move.
3. Draw a line around the region marked with Xs. This is the shape of the magnetic field. What does it show about the magnet?
4. (Optional) Repeat this procedure with a horseshoe magnet.

Bar magnet maglev?

Materials: Books, 2 rulers, string, binder clip, 2 bar magnets

1. Stand a bar magnet on a desktop. Have its north pole pointing up. Use books to hold the magnet in place.
2. Clip the binder clip to the south pole of the second bar magnet. Use the string to tie the clip closely to one end of the ruler, but loosely enough so that the magnet can swing freely.
3. Slowly position the ruler to bring the north poles of the two magnets together. Observe what happens.
4. Repeat step 3. Measure how far the dangling bar magnet can be lifted.

Dangerous fields?

Exposure to extremely strong electromagnetic fields, such as those from the world's most powerful magnets, can be dangerous or unhealthy. However, scientists agree that ordinary fields pose no health risk. Even the electric power lines that enter your home create only mild fields around them. You should NEVER touch, or even come close to, a downed power line. But the danger comes from electrical shock, not electromagnetic effects.

DISCOVER THE COMPASS

MATERIALS: COMPASS, BAR MAGNET

1. MOVE THE NORTH POLE OF A BAR MAGNET AROUND THE FACE OF A COMPASS. OBSERVE AND RECORD HOW THE NEEDLE MOVES.
2. REPEAT STEP 1 USING THE SOUTH POLE OF THE BAR MAGNET.
3. TAKE THE MAGNET TO A PARK OR PLAYGROUND. HOLD IT STEADY AS YOU WALK SLOWLY IN A CIRCLE. STOP WHEN THE NEEDLE POINTS NORTH.

SAFETY
CONSULT WITH YOUR TEACHER OR ANOTHER ADULT BEFORE YOU CONDUCT THIS ACTIVITY.

MAKE AN ELECTROMAGNET

Materials: Iron-containing nail or small rod, electrical wire, battery, metal paper clips

1. Wrap the electrical wire loosely around the nail, then connect its ends to the battery terminals.
2. Test the electromagnet on paper clips. Find out where the magnetic field is strongest and weakest, and the longest paper-clip chain it can pick up.
3. Repeat Steps 1 and 2, this time wrapping the wire tightly.
4. How else might you strengthen an electromagnet? Test your ideas.

Magnetism review

- **Magnetism** is a force that pushes or pulls on certain metals, including **iron**, **nickel**, and **cobalt**.
- In the **atoms** of magnetic **elements**, **electrons** are arranged in just the right way to create a magnetic force. The property may be lost when the atoms form **compounds**.
- Every **magnet** has two regions, called the north **pole** and the south pole, where the magnetic force is strongest.
- The north pole of one magnet will attract the south pole of another magnet. Two north poles will repel each other, as will two south poles.
- A **magnetic field** is the space in which a magnet's pull has an effect. It is strongest at the poles. Magnetic fields travel through solid, liquid, gas, and empty space.
- Earth acts as a giant magnet because of large amounts of iron and nickel in its core. A **magnetic compass** can show direction because it aligns to Earth's magnetic field.
- An **electromagnet** is a powerful, **temporary magnet** made by coiling a current-carrying wire around a piece of metal. It works because an **electric current** creates a magnetic field around it.
- Electromagnets are key parts of many devices, including sound speakers, **cathode ray tubes**, **motors**, and **generators**.

Glossary

atom smallest piece of an element, which is made of electrons and other particles

bar magnet magnet in the shape of a bar, with poles at opposite ends

cathode ray tube (CRT) tube that uses electromagnets to aim an electron beam at a screen. It is used in many television sets.

charged particle small particle with an electric charge

cobalt metallic element that is magnetic

code system of symbols used for communication

compound substance made from two or more elements joined together

crust hard outer layer of Earth

crystal type of material in which the atoms are arranged in an orderly pattern

Curie Point temperature above which a metal loses its magnetic properties

electrical transformer device for changing electric voltage

electric current flow of charged particles, such as electrons through a wire

electric field area surrounding an electric charge

electric motor device that uses electricity and magnetism to spin an axle

electromagnet strong temporary magnet powered by electricity

electromagnetic field combination of an electric field and magnetic field, created by any device that runs on electricity

electrons negatively charged particles of an atom

element substance that cannot be broken apart into simpler substances

friction force that slows down motion

generator device that uses magnets and a source of energy, such as rushing water or burning fuel, to make electricity

geographic poles ends of Earth's axis, labelled North and South

Global Positioning System (GPS) system that uses satellites and radio waves to pinpoint locations on Earth

horseshoe magnet magnet in the shape of a horseshoe, with poles at both ends

iron metallic element that is magnetic. It is used to make steel.

lava melted rock from Earth's interior that flows onto the surface or the ocean floor

lodestone magnetic mineral, made of a compound of iron and oxygen

Magnesia region of Turkey where lodestone, a magnetic rock, was discovered

magnet object that can push or pull by using magnetic force

magnetic compass device in which a magnetized needle points north, aligning to Earth's magnetic field

magnetic domain tiny region within a sample of iron or other metal, in which atoms are magnetically aligned

magnetic field area in which a magnet's pull has an effect. It is typically represented by lines and arrows.

magnetic field line lines that make up a magnetic field

magnetic levitation (maglev) process that uses magnets to lift something, such as a train

magnetic poles regions where the magnetic field is strongest, labelled North and South

magnetic resonance imaging (MRI) technique that uses powerful magnets and targeted radio waves to study the inside of the human body

magnetic shielding containing a magnetic field

magnetic tape plastic tape coated with a magnetic material such as ferric oxide. It is used to record sounds or data.

magnetism force that pushes or pulls on certain metals

magnetosphere region in space through which Earth's magnetic field reaches

Mid-Atlantic ridge the mid-ocean ridge in the Atlantic Ocean

mid-ocean ridge chain of underwater volcanoes that runs across the middle of each ocean

mu-metal alloy of iron, nickel, and other metals, used to shield a magnetic field

nickel metallic element that is magnetic

nuclei control centres of atoms. Nuclei is the plural of nucleus.

particle accelerator device that uses magnets and electricity to accelerate tiny particles, such as those that make up atoms

permanent magnet magnet that will keep its magnetic properties over time

plasma screen television screen made up of plasma, which is placed between two layers of glass and electrodes

power plant place where huge generators are used to make electricity and send it to a community

radio waves invisible waves that travel through air, space, and many other objects

rust compound of iron and oxygen

solenoid cylinder-shaped coil of wire, used in electromagnets

tectonic plate giant, moveable slab of Earth's crust

temporary magnet magnet that will lose its magnetic properties

volcano opening from Earth's interior to the surface, or the mountain that forms at this opening

x-ray form of electromagnetic radiation with great penetrating power

Further information

Books

Cutting Edge Medicine: Seeing Inside the Body, Andrew Solway (World Almanac Library, 2007)

Everyday Science: Opposites Attract: Magnetism, Steve Parker (Heinemann Library, 2005)

Magnetism and Electromagnets, Al Smuskiewicz (Heinemann Library, 2008)

Material Matters: Metals, Carol Baldwin (Raintree, 2006)

Websites

http://ippex.pppl.gov/interactive/electricity/

This interactive, hands-on site introduces you to the basic concepts involving electricity and magnetism.

http://www.bbc.co.uk/schools/ks3bitesize/science/physics/magnetism_intro.shtml

This site provides clearly set out information to aid revision about magnetism.

http://kids.earth.nasa.gov/archive/pangaea/evidence.html

Want to learn more about Alfred Wegener and his theory of continental drift? Go to this NASA site and find out why this scientist was on the cutting edge.

http://www.pbs.org/wnet/brain/scanning/mri5.html

Go on an MRI journey of the brain and learn how magnetism helps doctors view the most important part of the body.

Place to visit

Science Museum
Exhibition Road
South Kensington
London SW7 2DD
www.sciencemuseum.org.uk
Explore a museum dedicated to science!

Index